8/92   THE CHICAGO PUBLIC LIBRARY 13.95

DEC 1 0 1992	FEB 3 – 1995
DEC 1 0 1992	FEB 2 6 1995
JAN – 2 1993	JUN 1 1996
JAN 2 5 1993	OCT 2 4 1996
FEB 1 6 1993	FEB 1 3 1997 / MAR 0 4 1997
MAR 2 4 1993	MAY 1 3 1998
MAY – 7 1993	NOV 2 9 1999
MAY 2 6 1993	JUL 1 3 2000
FEB 1 4 1994	FEB 1 0 2001
APR 2 6 1994	
JUL 1 3 1994	
NOV – 1 1994	

FM 407 (1/86)

ANDROCLES AND THE LION
AND OTHER AESOP'S FABLES

RETOLD IN VERSE BY
TOM PAXTON

ILLUSTRATED BY
ROBERT RAYEVSKY

MORROW JUNIOR BOOKS
NEW YORK

Ink, watercolors, and acrylic were used for
the full-color art. The text type is 12 pt. ITC
Garamond Book.

Text copyright © 1991 by Tom Paxton
Illustrations copyright © 1991 by Robert Rayevsky

Printed in the United States of America.
1   2   3   4   5   6   7   8   9   10
Library of Congress
Cataloging-in-Publication Data
Paxton, Tom.
      Androcles and the lion and other Aesop's
fables/retold in verse by Tom Paxton ;
illustrated by Robert Rayevsky.
          p.   cm.
      Summary: A collection of Aesop's fables,
retold in verse, including "The Wolf in Sheep's
Clothing," "The Man, the Boy, and the Donkey,"
and "The Wolf and the Crane."
ISBN 0-688-09682-4 (trade).—
ISBN 0-688-09683-2 (library)
1. Fables.   [1. Fables.   2. Stories in rhyme.]
I. Rayevsky, Robert, ill.   II. Aesop's fables.
III. Title.
PZ8.3.P2738A7   1991
398.2—dc20
[E]   90-19173   CIP   AC

To Midge
—*T.P.*

Swiftly through the woods there ran
A slave named Androcles.
Breathlessly the young man ran
Beneath the spreading trees,
For Androcles had run away
From a harsh and cruel master,
And now he struggled through the woods.
Faster he ran—and faster.
Then all at once he heard a moan
Of something in great pain.
He stopped. He listened carefully,
And there! It came again.
Cautiously he felt his way
Until, at last, he saw
A mighty lion struggling
With a great thorn in his paw.
Again the poor beast groaned in pain,
Rolling his head about
Till brave young Androcles approached
And plucked the great thorn out.

At once the king of beasts sprang up
And licked the young man's hand,
But soon they both were captured
By the hateful master's band.

Then poor young Androcles was thrown
To the arena's sand.
The crowd was shouting down at him—
His end was near at hand.
The Emperor was seated,
And loud trumpets split the air.
A heavy gate was opened
And a hungry lion was there.
Spying poor trembling Androcles,
It raced across the sand
And, to the crowd's amazement,
Began to lick his hand.
It was the very lion
That the lad had helped before.
It stood beside young Androcles
And licked his hand once more.

Now, when the Emperor heard the tale,
He set the lion free;
And to kindhearted Androcles,
He granted liberty.
Both lion and lad won freedom;
The lesson we might learn
Is, when we help another,
He will help us in return.

The shepherd was watching his flock with such care,
The wolf couldn't get near the sheep that were there.
But one day the skin of a sheep the wolf found,
Discarded and left in a heap on the ground.
The wolf quickly put the sheep's skin on his back
And quietly moved to the midst of the pack.
A lamb he enticed to come wander away,
And that was his best meal in many a day.
Too late for the lamb, but for you and for me
Here's a moral: Don't always believe what you see.

A certain knight had lost his hair;
His flowing hair
Was no longer there.
To shelter his head from the cold night air,
A wig the old fellow wore.

One day as he went riding along
In a throng,
Singing a song,
There came a breeze quite fresh and strong,
And the wind at the red wig tore.
Whoosh! went the wind and snatched at the wig.
Jiggety-jig,
Away went the wig,
Off his old head, so shiny, so big,
As smooth as a marble stone.
"I can't expect," the old soul said,
Whose face was red,
"To keep instead
Another's hair upon my head,
If I can't keep my own!"

His friends could tease, his friends could chaff;
But this wise man knew how to laugh.

A mighty tree that stood on a hill
Said to a lowly reed,
"Dig your roots much deeper, child,
And make the world take heed
By stretching out your mighty limbs
Until they reach the sky.
For only then, my little reed,
Will you be as respected as I."
"I thank Your Honor—I certainly do,"
The lowly reed replied.
"And yet I feel I'm safer here;
So here I will abide."
"Safer!" snorted the mighty tree.
"Why, cast your eyes round here.
I am the tallest tree for miles;
So, whom have I to fear?"

But soon his answer he had, alas!
Too soon his answer he found:
A mighty hurricane ripped him up
And stretched him on the ground.
But the little reed bent to the wind
And lives in health today.
The reed didn't need to be king of the hill—
The reed knew when to give way.

THE DONKEY
CARRYING SALT

Down to the seashore went a man—
His donkey close behind.
He'd heard that salt was cheaper there
And a bargain he'd come to find.
He loaded the donkey with bags of salt—
As much as he could bear—
And drove the beast along the road
Beside a river there.
The donkey slipped, and down he slid;
He splashed into the stream.
Of course, the salt soon melted away
Like a fairy tale or a dream.
The donkey shook the water off;
He had no burden at all;
Without his load the donkey pranced
And danced home to his stall.

Back to the sea next dawn they went;
More salt was bought that day.
This time the donkey made *sure* to slip
And the salt went washing away.
Next morning they went to the shore again.
This time the master was smart:
A load of sponges he bought this time
And homeward they did start.
Now, when the donkey went into the stream,
Each sponge began to grow,
Till the donkey could neither stand nor swim;
His load had multiplied so.

Remember the donkey who lies in his coffin.
A trick can be played just once too often.

THE ANT AND THE DOVE

A thirsty ant stopped for a drink,
Where the stream came rushing down.
The current carried it swiftly away;
It seemed that it might drown.
A dove picked up a little twig
And dropped it near at hand.
The ant crawled onto the bobbing stick
And rode it safely to land.
Later a hunter was setting a trap—
The dove would be his prey.
The ant crept up and stung his leg,
And the hunter ran away.
Remember, sister!
Remember, brother!
One good turn deserves another.

THE KING OF THE BARNYARD

Two roosters were fighting each other;
Backward and forward they raged,
Causing a terrible ruckus—
What a great battle they staged!
Finally, one was the winner;
King of the barnyard was he.
The loser crawled under the hen house
And hid there where no one could see.
The winner flew up to a fence post—
The fire in his eyes brightly glowed;
He gazed at the scene of his triumph,
And, full of his victory, he crowed.
No one paid any attention;
The winner crowed louder, and then,
When, once again, nobody noticed,
He did it still louder again.

His noise reached the ears of an eagle,
Who cried, "It's my lucky day!"
He dropped from the sky like an arrow,
And carried that rooster away.

The moral is clear: The wisest folks know
That it's so nice to win, but it's foolish to crow.

A blue jay watched the peacocks pass;
He watched them strut across the grass.
He watched them proudly walk together—
He envied them each pretty feather—
And thought, "If only this poor jay
Could be as beautiful as they!"
Then, what was this? There on the ground
Some peacock feathers he had found.
He quickly tied them to his tail
And sped along the forest trail.
Some proud young peacocks soon he spied;
"Good morning, brothers!" loudly he cried.
They scorned this vain and foolish jay
And plucked the borrowed feathers away.

"Begone, you foolish bird!" they sneered.
"You're no peacock at all," they jeered.
The sad young blue jay flew away.
He'd had a most distressing day,
For shame and scorn were all he got
For trying to be what he was not.

THE MAN, THE BOY, AND THE DONKEY

An old man and his son
Led a donkey to the fair.
A stranger they encountered
Said they made a foolish pair.
"For look at you," the stranger jeered,
"A-walking side by side.
You have a healthy donkey here,
Which one of you could ride."

The old man climbed upon its back;
They went upon their way.
But then they met a second man,
And loudly he did say,
"Oh, what a cruel and selfish man!
Must you be so unkind?
You ride in comfort while the boy
Must tag along behind."

The old man climbed back down again
And now the young man rode.
They met another stranger,
And this stranger loudly crowed,
"How foolish to my eyes you seem.
It's clear, upon my oath,
That you've a healthy donkey
That could surely carry both."

So the old man rode behind the boy,
But they had not gone far
When still another stranger
Loudly cried, "How cruel you are!
I see your donkey's trembling limbs;
I see its pitiful eye.
With both of you upon its back
That beast is sure to die!"

So when the travelers reached the fair,
The people howled with glee,
For man and boy and donkey
Were a comical sight to see.
As down the road to town they came,
They staggered toward their goal,
For man and boy were carrying
The donkey on a pole!

They walked, they rode, they carried the beast;
They scurried on and off.
No matter what they tried to do,
Someone was sure to scoff.
So carve yourselves a wooden sign,
And place it on your shelf:
"You cannot please the world, and so
You'd better please yourself."

The greedy wolf was eating his fill,
Chomping and grinding away.
A little bone got stuck in his throat,
And he was heard to say,
"Won't someone pluck this wretched bone?
I cannot catch my breath!
Won't someone please remove the bone
Before I choke to death?"
He begged of everyone he met;
He pleaded—all in vain.
All creatures feared to help him
Till he met a friendly crane.
"Please help me, Mrs. Crane," he howled.
"I promise, if you do,
I'll give you quite a fine reward
To show my thanks to you."

The crane agreed, and with her bill
Reached in and plucked it out.
The wolf began to dance with glee;
He gave a happy shout.
"Excuse me, sir," the crane spoke up.
"You promised a reward."
The wolf began to smile at her;
Each tooth looked like a sword.
"Just be content, my friend," he snarled,
"And let good sense prevail.
You've had your head inside my mouth
And lived to tell the tale."